CONCU

How blue blocking
glasses can help heal your injured brain
by maximizing natural melatonin

DR. RICHARD L. HANSLER

ISBN: 1539867528
ISBN 13: 9781539867524
Library of Congress Control Number: 2016918472
CreateSpace Independent Publishing Platform,
North Charleston, South Carolina

CONTENTS

ACKNOWLEDGMENTS

Thanks go first to my wife, Wanda, for her patience and support as I continue to try to warn people of the dangers that lie in the use of light at night. I also want to thank my children and grandchildren for their support in encouraging me to continue doing what I love to do, well past normal retirement age.

Next I want to thank my partners in this business venture of providing products that not only help people sleep better but can aid in healing the brain: Dr. Edward Carome, Vilnis Kubulins, Daniel Carome, and Dr. Martin Alpert.

Special thanks to my daughter, Susan Thomsen, for editing the manuscript and son-in-law, Mark Thomsen, who designed the book cover.

INTRODUCTION

Concussion or mild traumatic brain injury (mTBI) occurs as a result of a sudden impact to the head and is one of the leading causes for visits to the emergency department. Concussions are most commonly due to falls, blows to the head, and motor vehicle accidents. Regardless of the cause, recovery from a concussion can be a slow process. This is not a medical book and it is of the utmost importance for you to follow your doctor's recommendations. This book will attempt to answer the question, "What else can I do to speed my recovery?"

In my earlier books, I examine the evidence that maximizing the natural production of melatonin by the pineal gland reduces the risk for diabetes, obesity, heart disease, Alzheimer's disease and breast, colon, and prostate cancer. Maximizing natural melatonin also improves sleep.

In this book, I begin with statistics regarding concussion. I then provide an extensive review of the scientific literature showing how maximizing natural melatonin may help to heal the damaged brain

I next examine how using ordinary light in the evening robs the body of melatonin and what can be done to fix the problem. Simple solutions are provided, by wearing orange glasses that block blue light or by using light bulbs that do not produce melatonin-suppressing rays. I also discuss when taking an oral melatonin supplement may be appropriate.

A current search of www.PubMed.gov (a government-funded medical abstracting website) with the words "Brain and "melatonin," produces 380 references. The earliest paper listed is by Dr. Charles Maurizi, a pathologist, now retired. In 1987, he warned that " *a chronic melatonin deficiency, with loss of dreams, could cause dementia.*" My warning, 29 years later, is "It may take your injured brain longer to heal if you expose your eyes to blue light in the evening when your body should be producing melatonin".

Rather than footnoting references, I have listed the PubMed Identification (PMID) number. Readers wishing to see the source of the information may go to the pubmed.gov website and type the number in the search box. In many cases a free copy of the entire paper is available for downloading. This website is a national treasure. Not as beautiful as a National Park, but well worth visiting, if you haven't been there.

CHAPTER 1

You are Not Alone

This year, 3 million kids from the ages of 6 to 14 are playing organized tackle football, according to USA Football. Even some 5-year-olds are in helmets playing in the Tiny Mite division of Pop Warner (which insists that its gladiators weigh at least 35 pounds). At the opposite end of the age spectrum, 50% of seniors over the age of 80 will experience a fall every year that may result in a concussion. Mild traumatic brain injury is a concern for all ages and stages of our lives.

This chapter presents statistics regarding the incidence of concussion.

From the Center for Disease Control (CDC):

Traumatic Brain Injury in the United States: Fact Sheet

Overview

Traumatic brain injury (TBI) is a major cause of death and disability in the United States, contributing to about 30% of all injury deaths. Every day, 138 people in the United States die from injuries that include TBI. Those who survive a TBI can face effects lasting a few days to disabilities that may last the rest of their lives. Effects of TBI can include impaired thinking or memory, movement, sensation (e.g., vision or hearing), or emotional functioning (e.g., personality changes, depression). These issues not only affect individuals but can have lasting effects on families and communities.

What is a TBI?

A TBI is caused by a bump, blow, or jolt to the head or a penetrating head injury that disrupts the normal function of the brain. Not all blows or jolts to the head result in a TBI. The severity of a TBI may range from "mild" (i.e., a brief change in mental status or consciousness) to "severe" (i.e., an extended period of unconsciousness or memory loss after the injury). Most TBIs that occur each year are mild, commonly called concussions.

How big is the problem?

- In 2010, about 2.5 million emergency department (ED) visits, hospitalizations, or deaths were associated with TBI—either alone or in combination with other injuries—in the United States.

  - TBI contributed to the deaths of more than 50,000 people.

  - TBI was a diagnosis in more than 280,000 hospitalizations and 2.2 million ED visits. These consisted of TBI alone or TBI in combination with other injuries.

- Over the past decade (2001–2010), while rates of TBI-related ED visits increased by 70%, hospitalization rates only increased by 11% and death rates decreased by 7%.

- In 2009, an estimated 248,418 children (age 19 or younger) were treated in U.S. EDs for sports and recreation-related injuries that included a diagnosis of concussion or TBI.

- From 2001 to 2009, the rate of ED visits for sports and recreation-related injuries with a diagnosis of concussion or TBI, alone or in combination with other injuries, rose 57% among children (age 19 or younger).3

What are the leading causes of TBI?

- From 2006–2010, falls were the leading cause of TBI, accounting for 40% of all TBIs in the United States that resulted in an ED visit, hospitalization, or death. Falls disproportionately affect the youngest and oldest age groups:

  - More than half (55%) of TBIs among children 0 to 14 years were caused by falls.

  - More than two-thirds (81%) of TBIs in adults aged 65 and older are caused by falls.

- Unintentional blunt trauma (e.g., being hit by an object) was the second leading cause of TBI, accounting for about 15% of TBIs in the United States for 2006–2010.

  - Close to a quarter (24%) of all TBIs in children less than 15 years of age were related to blunt trauma

- Among all age groups, motor vehicle crashes were the third overall leading cause of TBI (14%). When looking at just TBI-related deaths, motor vehicle crashes were the second leading cause of TBI-related deaths (26%) for 2006–2010.

- About 10% of all TBIs are due to assaults. They accounted for 3% of TBIs in children less than 15 years of age and 1.4% of TBIs in adults 65 years and older for 2006–2010. About 75% of all assaults associated with TBI occur in persons 15 to 44 years of age.

Risk factors for TBI

Among TBI-related deaths in 2006–2010:

- Men were nearly three times as likely to die as women.

- Rates were highest for persons 65 years and older.

- The leading cause of TBI-related death varied by age.

  - Falls were the leading cause of death for persons 65 years or older.

  - Motor vehicle crashes were the leading cause for children and young adults ages 5-24 years.

  - Assaults were the leading cause for children ages 0-4.

Among non-fatal TBI-related injuries for 2006–2010:

- Men had higher rates of TBI hospitalizations and ED visits than women.

- Hospitalization rates were highest among persons aged 65 years and older.

- Rates of ED visits were highest for children aged 0-4 years.

- Falls were the leading cause of TBI-related ED visits for all but one age group.

  - Assaults were the leading cause of TBI-related ED visits for persons 15 to 24 years of age.

- The leading cause of TBI-related hospitalizations varied by age:

    - Falls were the leading cause among children ages 0-14 and adults 45 years and older.

    - Motor vehicle crashes were the leading cause of hospitalizations for adolescents and persons ages 15-44 years.

End of CDC quote

From the "HeadCase" website:

Sports Concussion Statistics:

- 3,800,000 concussions reported in 2012, double what was reported in 2002

- 33% of all sports concussions happen at practice

- 39% -- the amount by which cumulative concussions are shown to increase catastrophic head injury leading to permanent neurologic disability

- 47% of all reported sports concussions occur during high school football

- 1 in 5 high school athletes will sustain a sports concussion during the season

- 33% of high school athletes who have a sports concussion report two or more in the same year

- 4 to 5 million concussions occur annually, with rising numbers among middle school athletes

- 90% of most diagnosed concussions do not involve a loss of consciousness

- An estimated 5.3 million Americans live with a traumatic brain injury-related disability (CDC)

End of "HeadCase" quote

Chapter 1 Summary

The statistics regarding concussion/mild traumatic brain injury speak to its widespread occurrence and potentially devastating impacts. Treatment for concussion has been widely studied with a variety of recommended approaches. The next chapter focuses on the scientific evidence that supports the role of melatonin in healing the injured brain.

CHAPTER 2

Scientific Evidence that Maximizing Natural Melatonin will Help Heal an Injured Brain

This chapter will provide a broad review of the scientific literature that addresses the role of melatonin in healing the injured brain.

Melatonin

Melatonin, chemically *N*-acetyl-5-methoxy tryptamine, is found in virtually every living organism from fungus to humans. It is a small molecule that can cross barriers (e.g. blood-brain barrier) that block larger molecules. In mammals, it is produced primarily in the pineal gland located at the base of the brain, near the center of the head. Its action as a hormone is by way of receptors located throughout the body. It also acts as both a direct antioxidant and as an indirect antioxidant by stimulation the production of antioxidant enzymes. Antioxidants protect cells by neutralizing reactive oxygen and nitrogen species, also called free radicals. The pineal gland is controlled by the internal clock. Production normally begins in the evening, the concentration increases to a maximum in the middle of the night and then drops to near zero about wake-up time.

Earliest study

The first (1997) study I could find that describes the benefit of melatonin in brain injury is titled, **"Cerebrospinal fluid melatonin in diseases of the nervous system"**, (PMID602555). It examined the concentration of melatonin in the spinal fluid that bathes the brain in 66 patients with some type of brain damage. They observed an increase in the concentration of melatonin and concluded that melatonin plays a defensive role in brain injury.

Recent study

A recent (2015) paper **"Melatonin attenuated early brain injury induced by subarachnoid hemorrhage via regulating NLRP3 inflammasome and apoptosis signaling"**, PMID26639408). As they put it, "In summary, our results demonstrate that melatonin treatment attenuates (reduces) the early brain injury following subarachnoid hemorrhage (bleeding in the brain) by inhibiting NLRP3 inflammasome-associated apoptosis (cell death). An inflammasome is a substance, produced by the body, that promotes inflammation and can cause cell death. Melatonin inhibits the inflammation caused by this substance and prevents cell death." A similar study by a different group also observed similar benefits from melatonin treatment.

In the 20 years between these papers, several hundred papers were written describing the benefit of melatonin in the case of brain injury. We will be discussing some of them, **but it is not necessary that the reader understand all the scientific terms in order to appreciate that there is a lot of evidence that having melatonin present in the injured brain is beneficial.**

The following literature review highlights some of the many areas of brain activity in which melatonin has been shown to have a protective and or healing effect.

Melatonin reduces neurological damage from head injury

- A 1998 paper (PMID9694403) from France is titled **"Protective effect of melatonin in a model of traumatic brain injury in mice"**. They found that giving melatonin injection 5 minute, 1,2,3 hours after head injury significantly reduced neurological damage, as measured by a grip test at 24 hours. They observed a protective effect and found it was not the result of a drop in core body temperature which is one effect of melatonin. They suggest the antioxidant power of melatonin may be responsible for the observed benefit.

- A 2014 paper from China (PMID24995391) is titled **"Melatonin reduced microglial activation and alleviated neuroinflammation induced neuron degeneration in experimental traumatic brain injury: Possible involvement of mTOR pathway."** These experiments were done with mice where extensive studies were made on the post-mortem brain. The results are included in the title. That more cells survived the damage is a significant result.

Melatonin reduces oxidative stress and prevents cell death

The term oxidative stress refers to damage to cells caused by free radicals. They are chemicals that are very reactive, that is, they are looking for things to react with. The two main kinds found in the body are reactive oxygen species (ROS) or nitrogen species. They are atoms or partial molecules that have unsatisfied bonds. Oxygen does not like to exist as an atom. That is, it wants to join with another atom and form a stable oxygen molecule (two atoms joined together). OH is another example. It wants to pick up another hydrogen and form H_2O. If melatonin (or other antioxidant) is present, it reacts with these active species so they don't damage the nerve cells. This is why you should eat your fruits and vegetables. They have lots of different antioxidants including melatonin. But melatonin is unique in that the pineal gland sends it directly into the brain as will be described in detail.

- In a paper from Turkey (1999) (PMID10702729) **"Melatonin as a free radical scavenger in experimental head trauma",** they found that secondary damage due to free radicals was reduced by melatonin injection but only if given in the first two hours.

- A 1997 study (PMID9030627) from the University of South Alabama is titled **"Melatonin Prevents Death of Neuroblastoma Cells Exposed to the Alzheimer Amyloid Peptide."** In this study we demonstrate that melatonin, a pineal hormone with recently established antioxidant properties, is remarkably effective in preventing death of cultured neuroblastoma (brain) cells as well as oxidative damage and intracellular $Ca2+$ increases induced by a cytotoxic fragment of Abeta.

- A paper from China (PMID24810171) is titled "**Melatonin stimulates antioxidant enzymes and reduces oxidative stress in experimental traumatic brain injury: the Nrf2-ARE signaling pathway as a potential mechanism"**. The administration of melatonin after TBI significantly ameliorated the effects of the brain injury, such as oxidative stress, brain edema, and cortical neuronal degeneration. Melatonin markedly promoted the translocation of Nrf2 protein from the cytoplasm to the nucleus; increased the expression of Nrf2-ARE pathway-related downstream factors, including heme oxygenase-1 and NAD(P)H: quinone oxidoreductase 1; and prevented the decline of antioxidant enzyme activities, including superoxide dismutase and glutathione peroxidase. (That's probably more than you wanted to know.)

- A 2015 paper from Turkey (PMID25339252) is titled, " **Reduction in traumatic brain injury (TBI)-induced oxidative stress, apoptosis, and calcium entry in rat hippocampus by melatonin: Possible involvement of TRPM2 channels."** Thirty-two rats were divided into the following four groups: control, melatonin, TBI, and TBI + melatonin groups.

Melatonin (5 mg/kg body weight) was intraperitoneally given to animals in the melatonin group and the TBI + melatonin group I h after brain trauma. Hippocampal neurons were freshly isolated from the four groups, and incubated with a nonspecific TRPM2 blocker. Cell death and many other undesirable factors were high in the TBI brains and low in the melatonin treated brains.

Less brain damage occurs at night due to increased melatonin

- In 2009, Russian scientists reported their observation that behavioral and morphological disturbances were less marked from head trauma in rats when the trauma is inflicted at night than during the day. They attributed this to the presence of melatonin during the night. Is this why night football has become so popular?

Melatonin is produced by the pineal gland during the night. A good question is "What is protecting the brain during the day?" A good answer might be "Melatonin and other antioxidants derived from the diet." This may be why it is important to eat those brightly colored fruits and a variety of nuts throughout the day, starting with breakfast

Melatonin reduces brain swelling (edema)

When the brain is injured, it tends to swell and the amount of spinal fluid increases. This increased pressure compounds the damage to the brain. This secondary effect of the injury may be more damaging than the initial blow.

- In a 2012 study from Turkey, (PMID23208906) melatonin was injected six hours after cortical impact injury in rats. (The cortex is the outer layer of the brain). Melatonin was observed to have a neuro-protective effect on secondary brain damage by significantly reducing brain edema (swelling).

- A related 2013 study (PMID23608674) from Iran is titled, " **Effect of melatonin on intracranial pressure and brain edema following traumatic brain injury: role of oxidative stresses"**. Melatonin was injected into the body cavity of rats at 1, 24, 48 and 72 hours after head trauma. The intracranial pressure and neurological scores were measured at similar times. Melatonin improved both. They attribute this to inhibition of oxidative stress.

Blood vessels are protected by melatonin

- Another paper from China (PMID25146619) is titled " **Microvascular protective role of pericytes in melatonin-treated spinal cord injury in the C57BL/6 mice."** Pericytes are contractile cells that wrap around capillaries. Melatonin ameliorated the loss of blood vessels and disruption of the blood spinal cord barrier to exert a protective effect, which might be mediated by increased pericyte coverage. The upregulation of Ang1 in pericytes could inhibit inflammation and apoptosis (cell death) to protect the microvessels. Damage to the pericytes can result in edema (loss of fluid from the blood vessels).

Benefits of melatonin for brain disease

Much of our knowledge of the brain and how it can be damaged comes from studies of diseases of the brain such as Parkinson's disease and Alzheimer's disease. The early signs are loss of memory and mild cognitive impairment. The fact that melatonin has been shown to be beneficial in these studies provides some of the evidence that melatonin may be helpful to a brain damaged in a concussion.

- Another 1997 paper **"Melatonin rescues dopamine neurons from cell death in tissue culture models of oxidative stress"** PMID9369331 describes how one type of brain neuron that is especially easily damaged, is protected, if melatonin is present. The neurons were grown in a culture in the laboratory. Dopamine neurons are well known because it is their absence from the brain that results in the symptoms known as Parkinson's disease. The protection of dopamine neurons by melatonin was confirmed in a 2002 study in the US (PMID11897104).

- A 2015 Indian paper (PMID25626558) is titled, **"Melatonin enhances L-DOPA therapeutic effects, helps to reduce its dose, and protects dopaminergic neurons in 1-methyl-4-phenyl-1,2,3,6-tetrahydropyridine-induced Parkinsonism in mice."** L-DOPA reduces symptoms of Parkinson's disease (PD), but suffers from serious side effects on long-term use. As a result of their study they concluded, prolonged, effective use of L-DOPA in PD with lesser side effects could be achieved by treating with 60% lower doses of L-DOPA along with melatonin.

Oral melatonin supplements reduce headache

Headache is a common result of mild traumatic brain injury (mTBI)).

- A 2013 study ((PMID23560811) at the University of Calgary, Alberta, Canada examined the effect of various drugs on headaches in children that occurred as a result of mTBI. They found, after two months, treatment with melatonin (3 -10 mg per day) resulted in complete relief in 9 out of 12 patients and partial relief in 2 of the 12.. One other drug (amitriptyline) had similar results while three others showed essentially no benefit.

Melatonin treatment reduces/reverses memory loss

An early sign of deterioration of the brain is the loss of short-term memory. Older people like to joke about a "senior moment" when they can't recall a name or a word for some common object. It is possible to simulate this effect by intentionally preventing sleep.

- In experiments in half a dozen different countries, short-term sleep deprivation in rats caused loss of both short- and long-term memory, activation of the neurons in the hippocampus, and chemical evidence of oxidative stress in blood samples. *Melatonin reversed or prevented all of these effects of sleep-deprivation-induced memory problems.*

- A 2015 paper (PMID25401971) from Korea found that mice subjected to chronic exposure to D-galactose (a form of sugar) suffered memory loss, synaptic dysfunction, elevated reactive oxygen species (ROS), neuroinflammation, and neurodegeneration. The results of treatment with melatonin are described as follows:

Our behavioral (Morris water maze and Y-maze test) results revealed that chronic melatonin treatment alleviated D-galactose-induced memory impairment. Additionally, melatonin treatment reversed D-galactose-induced synaptic disorder via increasing the level of memory-related pre- and postsynaptic protein markers. We also determined that melatonin enhances memory function in the D-galactose-treated mice possibly via reduction of elevated ROS and receptor for advanced glycation end products...Taken together, our data suggest that melatonin could be a promising, safe, and endogenous compatible antioxidant candidate for age-related neurodegenerative diseases.

- A very similar 2014 study (PMID24797165) in Taiwan found similar results. Researchers attributed the benefit to melatonin's ability to reduce oxidative damage.

- A 2015 paper (PMID25739489) from the Universidad de Colima, Colombia, describes the dynamic nature of the part of the brain that provides memory as follows:

Adult neurogenesis (formation of new neurons) in the dentate gyrus (DG) in the hippocampus is a process that involves proliferation, differentiation, maturation, migration, and integration of young neurons in the granular layer of DG. These newborn neurons mature in three to four weeks and incorporate into neural circuits in the hippocampus. There, these new neurons play a role in cognitive functions, such as acquisition and retention of memory, which are consolidated during sleep periods.

It thus appears that sleep deprivation interferes with this consolidation process and melatonin restores or prevents the damaging effect of sleep deprivation.

Sleep disruption is treated with melatonin

One result of mTBI can be damage to the pineal gland. If this happens and melatonin production is reduced, sleep problems may emerge.

- A 2015 paper from West Virginia University (PMID25956251) is titled "**Sleep disruption and the sequelae associated with traumatic brain injury.**" The abstract states in part "Sleep disruption, which includes a loss of sleep as well as poor quality fragmented sleep, frequently follows traumatic brain injury (TBI) impacting a large number of patients each year in the United States. Fragmented and/or disrupted sleep can worsen neuropsychiatric, behavioral, and physical symptoms of TBI. Additionally, sleep disruption impairs recovery and can lead to cognitive decline. The most common sleep disruption following TBI is insomnia, which is difficulty staying asleep. The consequences of disrupted sleep following injury range from deranged metabolomics and blood brain barrier compromise to altered neuroplasticity and degeneration." The suggested treatments are melatonin and cognitive behavioral therapy.

- A related paper from Louisiana State University (PMID25118920) is titled, **"Sleep in traumatic brain injury"**. The abstract states, "More than one-half million patients are hospitalized annually for traumatic brain injury (TBI). One-quarter demonstrate sleep-disordered breathing, up to 50% experience insomnia, and half have hypersomnia (excessive sleepiness). Sleep disturbances after TBI may result from injury to sleep-regulating brain tissue, non-specific neurohormonal responses to systemic injury, ICU environmental interference, and medication side effects. A diagnosis of sleep disturbances requires a high index of suspicion and appropriate testing. Treatment starts with a focus on making the ICU environment conducive to normal sleep. Treating sleep-disordered breathing likely has outcome benefits in TBI. The use of sleep promoting sedative-hypnotics and anxiolytics should be judicious." There is no mention of melatonin in the abstract but is listed as a keyword, suggesting it is an important treatment.

- .A 2014 study (PMID24555599) at the University of Pittsburgh is entitled, **"Evaluation of tentorial length and angle in sleep-wake disturbances after mild traumatic brain injury**." Patients with mTBI,. both with and without sleep problems, were studied using MRI to measure tentorial length and angle. They concluded that "Among patients with mild TBI with similar cognitive function and symptom severity, those with sleep-wake disturbances have significantly longer tentorial length with a flatter angle than do patients with mild TBI without sleep symptoms, with length of time to recovery being directly correlated with tentorial length and indirectly correlated with tentorial angle. *Direct impact between the tentorium and the pineal gland during mild TBI may lead to pineal gland injury, disruption of melatonin homeostasis, and sleep-wake disturbances.*" This suggests that if one has a mTBI and is experiencing sleep problems, check the MRI for tentorial length and angle and consider supplementing with melatonin by mouth.

- A 2014 paper (PMID24378071) from the UK is titled, **"Challenging behaviour and sleep cycle disorder following brain injury: a preliminary response to agomelatine treatment."** A single patient with severe brain injury had problems sleeping and behavioral problems. It was found that his circadian rhythm was not 24 hours long (N24). He was treated daily with agomelatine which improved his sleep and other problems.

- One of the few controlled studies of the benefit of melatonin in mTBI was done in a Russia in 2014 and is titled, **"Treatment of sleep disorders in patients with mild cranial-brain injury (CBI) in the early rehabilitation period"** To quote directly from the abstract:

MATERIAL AND METHODS:

Sixty patients were randomized to equal groups treated or not treated with melaxen (melatonin). Along with neurological and somatic examination, polysomnography and scales for measurement depression and quality of life (ESS, BDI, EuroQol etc) were used.

RESULTS AND CONCLUSION:

- Melatonin improved sleep (sleep latency, number of wakings per night etc)and decreased the severity of depression in the early rehabilitation period after mild CBI. Further research is needed to fully understand the effect of melatonin on sleep disorders in CBI, in particular in its later stages.

Melatonin prevents pesticide/heavy metal damage

- A 2014 study (PMID24733834) from India looked at the damage to cognitive function caused by a pesticide (Propoxur)
  and the effect of melatonin (MEL). Researchers concluded:
  "Treatment with MEL attenuated the effect of propoxur on
  oxidative stress. The results of the present study thus show
  that MEL has the potential to attenuate cognitive dysfunction and oxidative stress induced by toxicants like propoxur
  in the brain."

- A 2015 paper from China (PMID24969583) is titled,
  **"Melatonin inhibits manganese-induced motor dys-
  function and neuronal loss in mice: involvement of
  oxidative stress and dopaminergic neurodegeneration."** Mice were randomly divided into five groups as follows: control, MnCl2, low MLT + MnCl2, median MLT + MnCl2,
  and high MLT + MnCl2. Administration of MnCl2 (50 mg/kg)
  for 2 weeks significantly induced hypokinesis (slow movement), dopaminergic neurons degeneration and loss, neuronal ultrastructural damage, and apoptosis (cell death) in
  the substantia nigra and the striatum. They conclude that
  "Pretreatment with MLT attenuated Mn-induced neurotox-
  icity by means of its antioxidant properties and promotion
  of the DA system."

Melatonin prevents damage due to lack of oxygen

- A 2013 paper (PMID24399008) from Romania reported on
  the effect in rats of exposure to low atmospheric pressure.
  The lack of oxygen (hypoxia) causes cognitive and other
  damage that is reduced by having melatonin (MEL) in the
  blood. Researchers sum up their results as follows:

The most important morphological changes were observed in Group 2 (no MEL): increased cellularity, loss of pericellular haloes, shrunken neurons with scanty cytoplasm and hyperchromatic, pyknotic or absent nuclei; reactive gliosis, edema, and blood-brain barrier alterations could also be observed in some areas. MEL treatment significantly diminished all these effects. Our results suggest that melatonin is a neuroprotective antioxidant both in normoxia and hypobaric hypoxia that can prevent and counteract the deleterious effects of oxidative stress (neuronal death, reactive astrogliosis, memory impairment, and cognitive dysfunctions). Dietary supplements containing melatonin might be useful neuroprotective agents for the therapy of hypoxia-induced consequences.

- A more recent paper (PMID26443997) from Taiwan is titled " **Effects of melatonin on the nitric oxide system and protein nitration in the hypobaric hypoxic rat hippocampus.**" Rats were subjected to lack of oxygen by reducing the pressure to that found at 9000 meters' elevation. The conclusion states "Activation of the nitric oxide system and protein nitration constitutes a hippocampal response to hypobaric hypoxia and administration of melatonin could provide new therapeutic avenues to prevent and/or treat the symptoms produced by hypobaric hypoxia."

Other sources of melatonin within the body

- A 2014 study (PMID24554058) from Spain examined other sources of melatonin within the body.

With the aid of specific melatonin antibodies, the presence of melatonin has been detected in multiple extrapineal tissues including the brain, retina, lens, cochlea, Harderian gland, airway epithelium, skin, gastrointestinal tract, liver, kidney, thyroid, pancreas, thymus, spleen, immune system cells, carotid body, reproductive tract, and endothelial cells. Melatonin is present in essentially all biological fluids, including cerebrospinal fluid, saliva, bile, synovial fluid, amniotic fluid, and breast milk.

One might tend to think that the wide distribution of melatonin throughout the body diminishes the significance of the pineal-produced melatonin. The fact that it is the nightly flow of the pineal melatonin that controls not only the body temperature and many other circadian-rhythm-controlled processes but also the seasonal effects in many animals would suggest it is the pineal hormone that is the most significant for sleep and mental health. The direct connection between the pineal gland and the brain and the high concentration of melatonin in the spinal fluid suggest the melatonin produced in other parts of the body may not be important regarding its effect on the brain.

Benefits of the direct path of melatonin from pineal gland to brain

- The earliest study (PMID11751596) I could find on this subject was from France in 2002 and titled **"Melatonin enters the cerebrospinal fluid (CSF) through the pineal recess"**. There are cavities in the center of the brain called ventricles, two extending to the left and right sides of the brain and a third in the center. These cavities are filled with cerebrospinal fluid. An extension of the third ventricle reaches to the pineal gland. The experiments were done on sheep whose brain structure if very similar to the human brain. They sampled CSF from the volume next to the pineal gland (pineal recess) and within the main part of the third ventricle. The concentration of melatonin in the pineal recess was 1000 times higher than in the third ventricle. They concluded from this and related experiments that the pineal recess is the main site for penetration of melatonin into the

CSF.This explains how the concentration of melatonin in the CSF can be higher than in the bloodstream.

- An Italian 2007 paper (PMId17286741) is titled "**Ventricular cerebrospinal fluid melatonin concentrations investigated with an endoscopic technique**". Ten patients undergoing surgery for hydrocephalus were sampled for melatonin concentration in the ventricles and pineal recess. The concentration was highest in the third ventricle with no significant difference in the concentration in the pineal recess. No mention was made of the time of day of the surgery but most likely it was during the day when the pineal gland in not active.

- In a French study (PMID20004701) (2010) the concentration of melatonin in cerebrospinal fluid in patients with movement disorder was measured during surgery. They found the concentration of melatonin in the third ventricle was highest and higher than in the blood, in agreement with other studies.

- A study from France in 2014 (PMID24460899) measured melatonin (MLT) concentration in the cerebral tissue in the brains of sheep. The concentration was highest in the brain tissue adjacent to the ventricles with a gradient in concentration moving away from the ventricles. No such gradient was found for melatonin delivered through the bloodstream. Nocturnal concentrations were higher than daytime concentrations. They conclude "our data support the hypothesis that, in sheep and possibly in humans, only the CSF MLT, and not the blood MLT, can provide most of MLT to the cerebral tissue in high concentrations, particularly in the periventricular area".

- A 2014 study (PMID24553808) from the University of Texas describes the direct path from the pineal gland to the brain by way of the third ventricle. Melatonin concentrations in the CSF (spinal fluid) are not only much higher than in the blood, also, there is a rapid nocturnal rise at darkness onset and precipitous decline of melatonin levels at the time of lights on. Because melatonin is a potent free radical scavenger and antioxidant, we surmise that the elevated CSF levels are necessary to combat the massive free radical damage that the brain would normally endure because of its high utilization of oxygen, the parent molecule of many toxic oxygen metabolites, i.e., free radicals. Additionally, the precise rhythm of CSF melatonin provides the master circadian clock, the suprachiasmatic nucleus, with highly accurate chronobiotic information regarding the duration of the dark period. We predict that the discharge of melatonin directly into the 3V is aided by a number of epithalamic structures that have heretofore been overlooked; these include interpinealocyte canaliculi and evaginations (extensions) of the posterodorsal 3V that directly abut the pineal. Moreover, the presence of tanycytes (elongated cells)in the pineal recess and/ or a discontinuous ependymal lining in the pineal recess allows melatonin ready access to the CSF. From the ventricles melatonin enters the brain by diffusion and by transport through tanycytes. Melatonin-rich CSF also circulates through the aqueduct and eventually into the subarachnoid space. From the subarachnoid space surrounding the brain, melatonin penetrates into the deepest portions of the neural tissue via the Virchow-Robin perivascular spaces from where it diffuses into the neural parenchyma. Because of the high level of pineal-derived melatonin in the CSF, all portions of the brain are better shielded from oxidative stress resulting from toxic oxygen derivatives.

Despite the large number of unfamiliar names of the parts of the brain, the quotation conveys the important message that the direct path from the pineal gland to every part of the brain not only protects it from damage by free radicals, but provides accurate information about the duration of the dark period.

The importance of this direct path from the pineal gland to the brain cannot be overstated. In most of the studies cited above, melatonin was taken by mouth or injected and had to find its way to the brain via the intestines and bloodstream. A benefit was still observed despite this inefficient delivery system. Think how much bigger an effect one would see if the experiments had produced a 30% increase in melatonin injected directly into the brain from the pineal gland.

Another possible benefit of the direct path from the pineal gland to the brain is that hormones other than melatonin are also produced in this gland. In the 1990s the husband-and-wife research team of Bartsch and Bartsch (PMID11133007) found that these other hormones produced in the pineal gland were even more effective breast cancer fighters (antioxidants) than melatonin. Possibly the same may hold for the benefit to the brain. Again, it would seem that preserving the natural pineal production of melatonin and other hormones may help to heal an injured brain.

Chapter 2 Summary
The many different ways in which melatonin can help to heal a damaged brain have been described in technical papers from all over the world. The unique way it is directly injected into the brain by the pineal gland makes it obvious that maximizing natural melatonin production will be beneficial in recovering from concussion or mild traumatic brain injury.

If you are interested in even more scientific discussion of the benefits of melatonin, you may choose to read the entire paper (PMID25587567) published in 2015 by two Indian authors entitled **"Role of Melatonin in Traumatic Brain Injury and Spinal Cord Injury"**. It contains over 100 references. It does not, however, discuss how one can maximize natural melatonin by avoiding blue light in the hours before bedtime as will be discussed in Chapter 3.

CHAPTER 3

Circadian Rhythm, Melatonin, and Blue Light

What is Circadian Rhythm?

Most living things have some kind of internal clock. In humans, it is located in the hypothalamus in what is called the suprachiasmatic nucleus (SCN), at the base of the brain, near the center of the head. Because it is a 24-hour clock, it is also referred to as the circadian (about a day) clock. This clock is primarily controlled by special sensors in the retina of the eye called photosensitive Retinal Ganglion Cells (pRGC). These sensors are different from the rods and cones that produce vision. The pigment in them is called melanopsin and is also found in some frogs that change color. It absorbs blue light. Nerves from the pRGC go to the internal clock and to the part of the brain that partially controls pupil size, but not to the visual cortex where vision occurs. These blue light sensors were not identified until near the start of this century, thus explaining why most people are not aware of the importance of blue light in controlling the body. The blue rays in ordinary light affect both sleep and health and may stop the body from producing brain-healing melatonin.

Located next to the SCN is the pineal (shaped like a pine cone) gland. Melatonin is produced mainly under control of the circadian clock. When the eyes are exposed to light (especially blue light) first thing in the morning it restarts the circadian clock. Approximately 12 hours later the clock signals the pineal gland to start producing melatonin. The concentration in the blood and brain builds to a maximum about six hours later and then drops to near zero after another six hours. When the eyes are exposed to morning light, the sequence starts over again. This pattern very likely developed over millions of years as we evolved as humans. Most human evolution occurred near the equator where there are 12 hours of dark and 12 hours of light year-round.

The body's use of blue light to set the circadian clock worked perfectly until humans moved away from the equator. This resulted in the need to predict the changing weather conditions. The SCN then developed the capacity to not only serve as a clock but also as a calendar. As the periods of darkness grew longer in the fall, the fur bearing animals grew heavier fur, and in some cases, turned from brown to white. Some animals (possibly including humans) became fertile in the fall to have offspring in the spring when survival was highest. This was all mediated by when and for how long melatonin was present in the brain and in the blood stream. Once again, it all worked perfectly until electric lights entered the picture.

Artificial Light Bulbs and Blue Light
As artificial lights have evolved, the amount of blue light they produce has dramatically increased. This blue light has the capability of suppressing melatonin production and therefore disrupting our natural circadian rhythm.

The early forms of artificial light were flames (torches, candles, gas lights) that produced golden-colored light almost devoid of the blue rays that suppress melatonin production. Edison's original incandescent lamps had carbon filaments that could not be operated at very high temperature, again with relatively little blue light.

Each new generation of light bulbs has had more blue rays in their output. When the carbon filaments were replaced by tungsten, the temperature could be increased to make whiter light. Next came fluorescent lights, many of which were very blue.

White LED lights are actually a different kind of fluorescent light. The LED chip produces blue light, but is coated with a layer of phosphor that absorbs much of the blue light, which excites the phosphor to emit green, yellow, and red light. The combination appears as white light. The thickness of the phosphor coating controls how much blue light escapes. In general, LED light bulbs produce a larger fraction of blue light than incandescent bulbs.

Modern light bulbs have been tested to evaluate their effect on melatonin production. The energy output of a number of modern light bulbs was measured and multiplied by both the response curve of the sensors in the eye that control melatonin production (blue light component) as well as the response curve of the rods and cones that produce vision (total light component). The ratio of the blue light to total light components is reported as the "percent of melatonin-suppressing light".

The following table compares the melatonin-suppressing effects of several modern-day light bulbs:

Source Type	Percent Melatonin Suppressing Light	Lumen Output
Ecosmart 14W CFL 5000K 60W Equiv.	41%	922
GE Soft White 41W Halogen 2700K 60W Equiv.	31%	812
GE Soft White 60W Incandescent 2800K	29%	840
LS "Goodnight" 12W LED 2500K 60W Equiv.	22%	918
LowBlueLights 7W LED 1500K 25W Equiv.	4%	371

Note that even some of the bulbs that claim to be "low blue," such as the "Goodnight" bulb from Lighting Sciences, are not much lower than an ordinary incandescent bulb.

How Damaging is Lighting in Typical Homes?

The real question is whether the lighting found in most homes is capable of suppressing melatonin. Following is a review of the evidence that low levels of light (as found in a typical home) are sufficient to significantly reduce both the amount of melatonin and the time when it is present in the bloodstream and brain.

The basic unit of light is the lumen. It has the same dimensions as the watt. It is the rate of delivery of light energy. A burning candle produces four Pi (12.566) lumens. A lux is one lumen per square meter. If you hold a white paper one meter (39.37 inches) from a candle, it will give you an idea of what one lux looks like. It's pretty dim. Ordinary room light generally produces 180 lux or more, that is, it is sufficient to prevent the production of melatonin.

One of the most important studies in 2012 (PMID22017511) was financed by Philips, the world's largest producer of lights of all types, and carried out by the University of Surrey in the United Kingdom. They found that exposure to the types of lighting in the typical English home caused a significant increase in time to fall asleep and caused significant delays in the timing of the circadian rhythm. They confirmed that having more blue light increased the effect. This implies a decrease in melatonin production.

Harvard Medical School has conducted the most impressive studies of the effect of light on humans. Searching in PubMed with the three words "Harvard light melatonin" finds 85 papers starting in 1991. Charles Czeisler, MD, is the author of more than 230 papers and is probably the most prominent sleep scientist in the world. He is the head of the committee at the National Institutes of Health (NIH) concerned with sleep. My efforts to get NIH to conduct studies on the benefit of blocking blue light with orange glasses in the evening have not yet been successful.

In a 1998 study (PMID9579664), it was discovered that ordinary room light (180 lux) was sufficient to phase shift the circadian rhythm (change the setting of the internal clock) of melatonin and cortisol production and phase shift by the same amount the core body temperature rhythm. The body temperature drops to a minimum during the night, controlled by melatonin.

In 2000, a study (PMID10922269) of the effect of light intensity on circadian phase shift and melatonin suppression found intensity below about 80 lux had no effect, while above about 180 lux caused total suppression and significant phase shifting. This was before it was known that it is primarily blue light that suppresses melatonin, so we don't know how much blue light was in the sources used for these experiments. It must have been a relatively large fraction, as the light was from cool white fluorescent lamps.

In a 2007 study (PMID17502598), it was found that entrainment (locking in the circadian rhythm) to a daily schedule that was shifted by one hour could be accomplished by a daily exposure to as little as 100 lux of white light. An intensity of 25 lux had no effect. This shows again that the light levels found in homes are more than sufficient to have a major effect on the body.

A 2011 study (PMID21193540) found that evening exposure to moderate room light intensity (200 lux) experienced a delay in the start of the flow of melatonin and a reduction of about 90 minutes in the time that melatonin was present in the bloodstream.

A study at the Lighting Research Center in 2013 (PMID22850476) looked at the melatonin suppressing ability of an iPad tablet computer set at full brightness that delivered 40 lux at the eyes of 13 young-adult volunteers. After one hour there was a decrease in melatonin, but it did not reach statistical significance until after two hours. When the experiment was repeated with the subjects wearing orange glasses that block blue light, no melatonin suppression was observed.

A 2015 study (PMID25535358) at Harvard Medical School compared reading a book on a light-emitting e-reader with reading a traditional book in the hours before bedtime. The e-reader subjects experienced less same-evening sleepiness, took longer to fall asleep, and experienced phase delay in their circadian rhythm, suppression of melatonin, and decreased alertness the following morning.

Chapter 3 Summary

Blue light is important in controlling the daily flow of melatonin. The scientific studies just discussed demonstrate that even very moderate exposure to light in the hours before bedtime is able to significantly reduce the concentration of melatonin in the bloodstream and brain. It also significantly reduces the time when it is available. In order to maximize melatonin production, exposure to the blue-light component of artificial light must be reduced. Chapter 4 will examine how to avoid the damaging effect of light at night and consequently maximize the brain-healing benefits of increased melatonin.

CHAPTER 4

Avoiding Exposure to
Blue Light in the Evening
Can Help Heal Your Injured Brain

Chapter 2 examined how melatonin helps to heal the injured brain. Chapter 3 demonstrated the damaging effects of artificial light at night with regard to suppressing melatonin production. This chapter will provide simple, practical solutions for reducing exposure to blue light in the hours before bedtime.

The History of Low Blue Light Products

It has been known for many years that exposing the eyes to ordinary white light suppresses the production of melatonin. Most people who knew about it felt there was nothing to do about it, so why worry, even if it were bad for you. People were not going to give up using light in the evening or during the night.

That thinking changed when it was discovered in 2001 that it is mostly the blue rays in ordinary white light that cause melatonin suppression. When I learned this, I was very excited. Now we had a chance to get rid of the damaging effect of the millions of light bulbs I had helped develop at GE Lighting for more than forty years. I had a chance to deal with the guilt I felt for all the damage they had done to people's health.

I had retired from General Electric in 1996 and moved to John Carroll University in University Heights, Ohio, where I began studying the health effects of light. I became most alarmed when I learned (PMID11604480) that nurses who had worked night shifts for many years had double the incidence of breast cancer as compared to nurses who had not worked night shifts. This was consistent with an earlier study (PMID2054403) that found totally blind women had half the incidence of breast cancer as women with normal vision. In both cases melatonin was the link. Blind women had maximum melatonin because they did not lose theirs to light at night, while night shift nurses had less melatonin because of exposure to light at night.

When we learned that it was mainly blue light that was at fault, our team of physicists (Dr. Edward Carome and Vilnis Kubulins and I) went to work to develop light bulbs that did not make blue light and eyeglasses that block blue light. We had a number of failures initially, in which the coating we put on the bulb blocked blue light when new, but gradually became more transparent, probably from running at too high a temperature. We finally succeeded in getting some reliable products and opened a website in July of 2005 where we made these products available to the public.

Low Blue Light Bulbs and Eyeglasses

In addition to making Low Blue light bulbs, we determined, early on, that it really didn't matter where you blocked the blue rays, whether it was where they came out of the bulb or in front of the eyes. We began looking for eyeglasses that blocked only the blue rays, since we didn't want to prevent people from carrying on their normal evening activities such as working on a computer, watching TV, or reading. We determined we needed to provide two types of glasses, one we called "fitover" glasses that were large enough to be worn on top of reading glasses and those we called "nonfitover" for those not requiring read-ing glasses. We quickly found people want to look good when wearing them, so we searched to find manufacturers who would provide fashion frames that were then equipped with the orange lenses required to block the blue rays.

Thousands of people have bought our glasses with a guarantee of money back if they did not improve their sleep. Based on the small number who find they do not help and return the glasses, we estimate they help more than 90% of those who try them. This is a much higher number than that for sleeping pills. Unlike sleeping pills, whose effectiveness wears off after a time, there is no such effect with maximizing natural melatonin. Using glasses that block blue light (from any source, natural or artificial) in the evening or using light bulbs that don't make blue light, restores the conditions we experienced as human beings when we evolved. We evolved near the equator, where there are 12 hours of light and 12 hours of darkness year-round. Blocking blue light makes your body act as if in darkness. We sometimes call it virtual darkness.

As a person with a pension from GE Lighting, I was concerned that the company was continuing to make what I considered to be an unsafe product. I kept urging my contacts at GE to provide light sources without blue light for use in the evening. I'm not sure if it was my urging or if it was the arrival of the "Goodnight" bulb from Lighting Sciences that convinced them to develop a pair of light bulbs they are calling "Align AM" and "Align PM." The first has extra blue light to reset the internal clock in the morning and suppress any remaining melatonin, and the second has reduced blue light. They made the PM version less likely to reduce melatonin production in the evening by reducing both the intensity and the fraction of blue light. In tests with consumer groups, they found that completely removing the blue, that is, making it an orange light, would not be well accepted by customers. This has not been our experience with our orange bulbs. People love the peaceful color that resembles candlelight. Our customers want light free of the blue rays, but it must be bright enough that they can carry on their normal evening activities, such as reading.

Recently GE announced a website www, CbyGE.com where light bulbs are described that can have their color adjusted to provide lots of blue light in the morning and during the day and can become low in blue light in the evening and during the night.

Blue Light Blocking Filters for Screens

Since the time we started our website, mobile devices such as iPads and iPhones have become common. Their screens provide a lot of blue light. People take these devices to bed with them, sometimes keep using them until very late, and sometimes look at them during the night. This can raise havoc with their sleep. Two members of our team, Daniel Carome and Vilnis Kubulins, developed a line of flexible, thin, vinyl filters that block blue light. They can be placed on the screens without interfering with the touch screen requirements. They adhere tightly to the smooth surface without any need for an adhesive. If they get dirty they can be restored to new condition with soap and water. Other filters for notebooks and laptop computers have been developed that use a heavier rigid plastic.

Websites and Apps

For many years there has been a free program available called Flux that adjusts the color of computer screens to orange in the evening. Now there are apps available for smart phones that do the same. Apple is the latest to join by providing "nightshift" for their devices.

Use of Low Blue Light Products for Concussion

It would have been nice if 10 years ago (or even just a year ago), we had recruited 200 people with concussions, randomized them into two groups, and started an experiment. One group would wear orange glasses every evening for three hours before bedtime, and the other group would wear colorless glasses for the same time. Today we might be able to report the results of tests of recovery from concussion in the two groups.

Unfortunately, such a simple test is not possible. To do the simplest experiments on humans in the United States, even just filling out a medical questionnaire, one has to have the plan approved by an internal review board (IRB), and the participants have to sign an informed consent form. It seems like a good idea, but the IRB has become a major impediment to finding simple answers to simple questions.

For now, we must be content to give the evidence that:

(1) **maximizing melatonin appears to help the healing of an injured brain.**

(2) **exposure to light in the evening suppresses melatonin.**

(3) **blocking blue light in the evening with orange glasses or special lightbulbs or filters restores the flow of melatonin.**

Therefore, using LowBlueLight products in the evening may help to heal an injured brain.

Perhaps clinical trials of the glasses will be done someday. I hope so, but it is not likely during my or your lifetime. Fortunately, the reader is not constrained by the need for clinical trials. Most reasonable people will accept logic as sufficient for action. Without action, knowledge has little value.

Because the use of LowBlueLight products will enhance sleep and reduce the risk of many other diseases and conditions, it seems like it might be worth the bother.

Further Evidence for the Benefits of Low Blue Light Products

If you are still not convinced to switch to LowBlue light bulbs or orange glasses, perhaps this will convince you…

The only light bulbs and eyeglasses that truly remove all of the light rays that are known to be responsible for melatonin suppression are the ones available at our website www.lowbluelights.com. I mention our competitors only to convince you that it's not just us that recognize the problem.

GE Lighting has provided a careful study of available medical information about the effect of light on sleep that the reader can check on their website at http://www.gelighting.com/LightingWeb/align/images/GE-Lighting-And-Sleep-Whitepaper.pdf

Further reason to take action is in the statement from this Florida-based lighting company:

> Lighting Science Group (OTCQB:LSCG), one of the world's top developers of LED lighting solutions, announced today_that it would begin putting labels on light bulbs alerting consumers to the potential link between health and lighting products—specifically highlighting how exposure to electric lights prior to bedtime may cause sleep disruption and other effects.

> The new initiative is receiving broad support from the scientific and medical communities. Former US Secretary of Health and Human Services Dr. Louis W. Sullivan, MD, applauded the effort, saying: "Providing helpful information to the public is important and necessary to protect and enhance the health of our citizens. Many studies have found that lighting has a significant biological effect—impacting sleep, alertness, and many other physiological functions." A 2014 research report released by Harvard Medical School concluded "the use of portable light-emitting devices

immediately before bedtime has biological effects that may perpetuate sleep deficiency and disrupt circadian rhythms, both of which can have adverse impacts on performance, health, and safety."

"The effect of light on human health and wellness is meaningful and well documented," said Fred Maxik, founder and chief technology officer of Lighting Science. "We decided it was time to be proactive and raise awareness of those effects. This warning actually belongs on all light bulbs produced worldwide, and we'd hope that other lighting developers and manufacturers will join us in adding similar labels to their products."

"This is an issue that needs and deserves much greater attention," said Dr. Michael Breus, one of the nation's leading authorities on clinical sleep disorders and who is also known as "the Sleep Doctor."

"Light affects our biology, our performance, and our psychology. Like any powerful medicine, we need to use caution, education, and experience in choosing what type of light is right for different situations and when is the best time to use it."

Lighting Science has always placed a strong emphasis on science and technology-based lighting solutions. The company initially garnered attention through its partnership with NASA, designing lights to improve the alertness and sleep patterns of astronauts on the International Space Station. "Lighting Science Group views our role in much broader terms than simply a traditional lighting company," said chairman Craig Cogut. "Our focus is the impact of lighting on health, and we are using new scientific findings and technological advances as the basis for product development." Lighting Science's Rhythm Series leverages the company's focus on sleep improvement with biologically oriented products such as the Sleepy Baby and Good Night lights. The company's scope of products has expanded in recent years to include the Avenue Series, which focuses on outdoor lights for communities and roadways; the Marquee Series, filament bulbs inspired by vintage designs; and a variety of other products that seek to address issues in the realms of agriculture, wildlife protection, and energy efficiency. "It's a revolutionary time for Lighting Science," said CEO Ed Bednarcik. "We want to lead the way in helping to inform customers, as well as providing solutions for utilizing light more effectively and safely." The first new labels will begin appearing on packages in specific channels later this summer (2015), with a full rollout planned in the following months. For more information on the biological effects of light, please, please visit http://www.healthimpactoflight.com/.

The very powerful effect that light has on the human brain was demonstrated in a recent study in Norway by Dr. Leon Henriksen in which she used our Lowbluelights orange glasses to treat bipolar disease patients that had been hospitalized because of mania. The study was carried out in three different hospitals over a period of over a year. Patients were provided at random with either the orange glasses or similar glasses with clear lenses. The patients wore the glasses in the period both before and after sleep in darkness to give a total time of 14 hours. Every one of the patients with the orange glasses showed improvement in only a few days and were better after only a week. The patients receiving the clear glasses showed little improvement. The glasses were in addition to treatment as usual. Typical recovery from mania is a matter of months.

Whether it is the result of making more melatonin available is not clear at this point. It seems likely that something more basic is involved. It is well known that light, especially blue light, stimulates the brain and increases production of cortisol and adrenaline. Perhaps it is the lack of this stimulation that happens when wearing the glasses, that allows the mania to subside.

It seems likely that this same lack of stimulation achieved by wearing orange glasses, would be helpful for an injured brain. While darkness would achieve the same benefit, people are not willing to spend 14 hours in darkness.

Future Research

The following abstract describes a clinical trial that was recruiting at the time I wrote this (August 2016). I think it will be the first controlled study to determine whether maximizing melatonin will be beneficial to an injured brain.

Trials. 2014 Jul 7;15:271. doi: 10.1186/1745-6215-15-271.

A double-blind, placebo-controlled intervention trial of 3 and 10 mg sublingual melatonin for post-concussion syndrome in youths (PLAYGAME): study protocol for a randomized controlled trial.

Barlow KM[1], Brooks BL, MacMaster FP, Kirton A, Seeger T, Esser M, Crawford S, Nettel-Aguirre A, Zemek R, Angelo M, Kirk V, Emery CA, Johnson D, Hill MD, Buchhalter J, Turley B, Richer L, Platt R, Hutchison J, Dewey D.

Author information

- [1]Alberta Children's Hospital Research Institute, University of Calgary, Room 293, Heritage Medical Research Building 3330 Hospital Drive NW, Calgary, AB T2N 4N1, Canada. Karen.barlow@albertahealthservices.ca.

Abstract

BACKGROUND:

By the age of sixteen, one in five children will sustain a mild traumatic brain injury also known as concussion. Our research found that one in seven school children with mild traumatic brain injury suffer post-concussion syndrome symptoms for three months or longer. Post-concussion syndrome is associated with significant disability in the child and his/her family and yet there are no evidence-based medical treatments available. Melatonin has several potential mechanisms of action that could be useful following mild traumatic brain injury, including neuroprotective effects. The aim of this study is to determine if treatment with melatonin improves post-concussion syndrome in youths following mild traumatic brain injury. Our hypothesis is that treatment of post-concussion syndrome following mild traumatic brain injury with 3 or 10 mg of sublingual melatonin for 28 days will result in a decrease in post-concussion syndrome symptoms compared with placebo.

METHODS/DESIGN:

Ninety-nine youths with mild traumatic brain injury, aged between 13 and 18 years, who are symptomatic at 30 days post-injury will be recruited. This study will be conducted as a randomized, double blind, placebo-controlled superiority trial of melatonin. Three parallel treatment groups will be examined with a 1:1:1 allocation: sublingual melatonin 3 mg, sublingual melatonin 10 mg, and sublingual placebo. Participants will receive treatment for 28 days. The primary outcome is a change on the Post-Concussion Symptom Inventory (Parent and Youth). The secondary outcomes will include neurobehavioral function, health-related quality of life and sleep. Neurophysiological and structural markers of change, using magnetic resonance imaging techniques and transcranial magnetic stimulation, will also be investigated.

DISCUSSION:

Melatonin is a safe and well-tolerated agent that has many biological properties that may be useful following a traumatic brain injury. This study will determine whether it is a useful treatment for children with post-concussion syndrome. Recruitment commenced on 4 December 2014.

TRIAL REGISTRATION:

This trial was registered on 6 June 2013 at ClinicalTrials.gov.

REGISTRATION NUMBER:

NCT01874847.

CHAPTER 5

Oral Melatonin Supplements

Chapter 2 outlined the evidence that melatonin may be beneficial to an injured brain. If you or a loved one have had a blow to the head, avoiding blue light in the evening and during the night in order to maximize melatonin is a reasonable course of action. You should inform your doctor and follow his or her advice.

While avoiding blue light in the evening will help your body to maximize it's natural melatonin production, there is a wide range in the amount of melatonin produced by different people. For this reason, some people will want to supplement their own melatonin with melatonin taken by mouth or by eating melatonin-rich foods.

Oral Supplements

The first question that needs to be considered is whether it is safe. In a review paper from the University of Adelaide, South Australia (PMID25643981), the reasons for questioning the safety of oral melatonin supplements for children are raised as follows:

(i)   it is not registered for use in children anywhere in the world;

(ii)   it has not undergone the formal safety testing expected for a new drug, especially long-term safety in children.

(iii) it is known to have profound effects on the reproductive systems of rodents, sheep, and primates, as well as effects on the cardiovascular, immune, and metabolic systems; and

(iv) there is the potential for important interactions with drugs sometimes prescribed for children.

Dr. Rusell Reiter, who literally wrote the book on melatonin (*Melatonin*, Bantam Books, 1995), has enumerated hundreds of diseases and conditions where melatonin is beneficial. He does not mention conditions where it is damaging. However, it is a powerful substance and, if used at the wrong time of day or season of the year, might have unexpected effects. For example, I described at one time that natural fertility increases as the nights are increasing in length (longer flow of melatonin) and suggested that putting on our orange glasses a few minutes earlier each night might improve chances of conceiving. A few months later I received a letter thanking me and saying it had worked for this couple. Taking melatonin by mouth a little earlier each night might have a similar effect, which might or might not bring joy, depending on the circumstances.

In searching PubMed.com for "contraindications for melatonin," I did not find any results pointing out problems. When used as a sleeping aid, next-day drowsiness is a complaint, and headaches are sometimes mentioned.

The biggest question is whether any melatonin taken by mouth will end up in the brain. The answer would seem to be yes. While many of the studies described in chapter 2 were about internally-produced melatonin, many also reported on having used oral melatonin.

One of the things holding up the use of melatonin in the treatment of mTBI is the fact that melatonin is not a controlled substance in the US, has never been approved by the FDA and is regarded as a food supplement by the US government. One cannot get a prescription for melatonin in the US. On the other hand, melatonin agonists (chemically similar material) have been developed and patented and some have been approved by the FDA.

This raises the question of whether some of the melatonin agonists (drugs having a chemical structure nearly identical to melatonin and having similar effects on the body) might be more effective than melatonin. Since people haven't figured out how to make money by doing clinical trials of melatonin (or using orange glasses to maximize it), there is hope the agonist makers might carry out clinical trials. Since their drugs are patented, they can charge a lot if they can show their drug helps in healing an injured brain.

The oldest melatonin agonist is Circadin and may actually be melatonin (the patent relates to its slow-release formulation). It is described by the manufacturer as follows:

> Circadin, a novel prolonged release formulation, is able to mimic the internal melatonin secretion profile by releasing melatonin gradually over 8–10 hours from the time it's is being swallowed.
>
> In well-controlled clinical trials in thousands of insomnia patients, Circadin has been proven to help patients to fall asleep easily and have a good night's sleep, allowing them to wake up feeling refreshed and ready for the next day.
>
> Circadin is the first sleep agent to demonstrate improvements in next-day functioning and quality of life and is the only licensed medication containing melatonin.
>
> Because of its proven efficacy and long-term safety, Circadin is the only sleep drug approved for treatment for up to 13 weeks, without being restricted to several days as other insomnia drugs.

Because Circadin makes melatonin available in the blood stream in a manner similar to the way it is produced by the pineal gland, it may be a valid way to help heal an injured brain. Other melatonin agonists are romelteon, agomelatine, tasimelteon (Hetlioz), and TIK-301.

It would be hugely beneficial if the pharmaceutical companies would conduct clinical trials to prove the benefits of maximizing melatonin for preventing breast cancer or obesity or dementia and Alzheimer's disease or of helping to heal an injured brain. I would recommend the latter since the results would be evident in a matter of weeks or months, not many years.

Food Sources of Melatonin
The following is from the Natural Society.

> There are several foods, however, that can naturally increase melatonin production, eliminating the need for a supplement. According to GreenMedInfo, researchers with Thailand's Khon Kaen University found that some tropical fruits have significant effects on melatonin production. The scientists gave study subjects a variety of fruits and then measured the amount of melatonin circulating throughout the body by looking at 6-sulfatoxymelatonin (aMT6s).

> The researchers found pineapples, bananas, and oranges were able to increase melatonin presence significantly. Pineapples increased the presence of aMT6s over 266% while bananas increased levels by 180%. Oranges were able to increase melatonin by approximately 47%.

> While supplements are often thought of as the natural alternative to prescription drugs, they are made to mimic those things we find naturally in foods. In other words, they too are a poor substitute for good nutrition and some supplement manufacturers

(though not all) are in the business to make money, not with noble intentions of increasing the collective health.

Some Melatonin-Boosting Foods:

Pineapples

Bananas

Oranges

Oats

Sweet corn

Rice

Tomatoes

Barley

Chapter 5 Summary
The potential benefits of oral melatonin supplements are best described by Dr. Tan:

"Evaluation of the melatonin levels in tissues and other body fluids based on the blood melatonin concentrations appears to be inadequate since the distribution of melatonin in the body is not homogenous. Several studies have shown that levels of melatonin in CSF (spinal fluid) are much higher than those in the blood. Evidence indicates that melatonin originating from the pineal gland and melatonin synthesized by brain tissue both contribute to the high level of melatonin in CSF. The major source of melatonin in CSF seems to come from the direct release of melatonin from the pineal gland into the pineal recess of the third ventricle. This leads to a melatonin concentration gradient in CSF as the fluid flows through the ventricular system including the aqueduct, fourth ventricle, and subarachnoid space. Melatonin in the CSF is speculated to protect the surrounding brain structures from oxidative and nitrosative stress. A low level of melatonin in CSF may relate to the etiology of neurodegenerative diseases which have elevated oxidative stress, e.g., Alzheimer disease. Decreased melatonin levels in CSF have been observed in patients with this neurodegenerative condition. Long term melatonin supplementation may retard the progress of some neurodegenerative diseases. This conclusion is based on a variety of animal studies and several small scale clinical investigations."

CHAPTER 6

Conclusion

Perhaps it will be helpful to step back and look at the big picture instead of the details. What we can conclude is that:

1. There is strong evidence that providing the brain with melatonin is beneficial in healing an injured brain.

2. There is also clear evidence that even moderate levels of light, especially blue light, can suppress evening/nighttime melatonin production.

3. There are light bulbs available that do not make blue light and glasses and filters available that block blue light. The use of these Low Blue Light products will restore the body's natural melatonin production.

4. Maximizing natural melatonin production by the pineal gland is more effective than taking melatonin by mouth because of the direct connection from the pineal gland to the brain.

5. A regular daily schedule for getting up, exposing the eyes to light, eating, exercising, avoiding blue light in the evening, and going to bed is likely to improve recovery from concussion.

6. This life-style may also improve your sleep and reduce your risks for diabetes, obesity, heart disease, and breast, colon and prostate cancer.

38755076R00033

Printed in Great Britain
by Amazon